REAL-LIFE STORIES

FOR ADVANCED BEGINNERS

Edited by
Grace Massey Holt
Fiona Chin
Barbara Bowers

Dominie Press, Inc.

Publisher: Raymond Yuen
Project Editor: Becky Colgan
Text Illustrations: Tony Greven
Cover Design: Pamela Pettigrew-Norquist

Published by:

Dominie Press, Inc.

1949 Kellogg Avenue
Carlsbad, California 92008 USA

www.dominie.com

1-800-232-4570

ISBN 1-56270-235-1
Printed in the U.S.A.
4 5 6 7 8 9 10 VO88 10 09 08 07

Table of Contents

Introduction

Real-Life Stories was written for the adult ESL student. This book reflects the diversity of the needs and interests of these students. The stories were written and chosen for their multicultural appeal in an American context. Each unit contains a pre-reading section with a picture, vocabulary, and often some pre-reading questions. This is followed by the story, comprehension questions, and exercises.

This book is designed to be used as supplementary reading material by students in a classroom situation with an instructor. It may be adapted for the independent use of students in a self-access learning center, for example, but input from an instructor will be necessary. The pre-reading section is intended to activate students' prior knowledge of the topic, introducing essential vocabulary and generating discussion. The exercises in the chapters vary in levels of difficulty. Some of the exercises might be too challenging for a high beginning or low intermediate class. However, these exercises were field tested quite successfully by instructors who had highly motivated and enthusiastic students at those levels. The exercises are a mixture of the easy and familiar, the interactive and fun-to-do, and the challenging. It is up to each instructor to decide which of the exercises his or her class is capable of and will enjoy. This might be useful to instructors of a multilevel class where different exercises could be assigned to different students.

Suggested Procedure

Pre-reading (first page of each lesson)

1. Ask the class to look at the top of the page and read the title of the lesson.
2. Ask students for suggestions on what they think the story (lesson) will be.
3. Give students time to look at the picture, the vocabulary, and the question(s) following the picture.
4. Write the vocabulary on the board. Elicit definitions for each word or phrase. Write the definition after each vocabulary item. Next, ask volunteers to make sentences with each vocabulary item. Write each sentence on the board next to the definition.
5. Discuss the question(s).

Reading the Story (top of second page of each lesson)

6. Model read the story two times as students follow in their books.
7. Ask students to read the story silently and underline any words they do not know.
8. Ask students to tell you the words they have underlined as you write each on the board.
9. After all the words have been listed on the board, elicit as many definitions as possible from the students. Go over the meaning for each word. Ask volunteers to make sentences with the words.
10. Model read the story one more time.

Comprehension Check

11. As students look at the story, ask several questions from each of the following categories:
    a. *Yes/No* questions: Questions that require a *yes* or *no* answer.
    b. Alternative or *either/or* questions: Questions in which a choice for the answer is given.
    c. Information or *Wh—* questions: Questions that ask for information regarding *who, what, when, where, how much/many, how, why.*
    d. Inference questions: Questions that require students to suppose an answer based on the content of the story.
    e. Real-life questions: Questions that require students to answer based on their own lives.

By asking questions using the above order, you move from the simplest (*yes/no*, alternative questions) to the more difficult (information, inference questions) to students' life experiences.

The following example provides a sample question from each category based on one sentence.

Janet bought a carton of milk on Saturday.

   a. *Yes/No* question: Did Janet buy a carton of milk on Saturday?
   b. Alternative question: Did Janet buy milk or juice?
   c. Information question: When did Janet buy milk?
   d. Inference question: Does Janet like milk?
   e. Real-life question: Do you like milk? Do you buy milk?

Skimming for Information

12. *True/False:* Read each sentence, either as it is written or with some change. If the sentence is correct, the class indicates this by saying *true*. If the sentence is not correct, the class indicates this by saying *false*. After going through the story one time, read the story a second time. This time read the sentences out of sequence and make a change in each one. Ask students to find the correct sentence and read it back to you as it is written in the book.

     Example: *Janet bought a carton of milk on Saturday.*

    First Reading

Teacher:	Janet bought a carton of juice on Saturday.
Students:	False
Teacher:	Janet bought a carton of milk on Sunday.
Students:	False
Teacher:	Janet bought a carton of milk on Saturday.
Students:	True

    Second Reading

Teacher:	Janet bought a bottle of juice on Sunday.
Student Volunteer:	Janet bought a carton of milk on Saturday.

13. *Read/Stop.* Read the story. Tell students that you will stop at certain points in the story. When you stop, students should read the next word. After doing one-word deletions, you may want to repeat the exercise with two-word deletions.

Using Contextual Clues

14. *Oral Close:* Ask students to turn their books over so they cannot see the story. Read the story as students listen. When you come to context words, pause for the students to fill in the missing word. Allow any word that makes sense within the context of the story, even though it may not be the actual word in the story. Go through the story two or three times, leaving out different words each time.

Comprehension Questions (bottom of second page)

15. Ask students to write the answers to the questions that are on the second half of the page. Encourage them to look for the answer in the story, if they cannot remember.
16. Ask volunteers to read the question and answer, or ask volunteers to write the answers on the chalkboard.

Exercises (remainder of lesson)

17. Presentation and practice for exercises will depend on you and your class. Some exercises may need extensive introduction, explanation, and oral practice before students can complete them. Others will need no explanation at all. How each is completed will depend on the level of your class and your teaching style.

Sour Milk

Vocabulary

sour   apologized

check-out   problem

understanding

Janet had a problem this morning. She bought a carton of milk on Saturday. However, when she opened it this morning, the milk was sour. She took it back to the store. The check-out clerk apologized and was very friendly. She changed the carton for a fresh one. Janet was happy that the carton of milk was changed so quickly. The store owner and check-out clerk were very understanding.

Comprehension Questions

1. What did Janet do on Saturday? _____

   _____

2. What was wrong with the milk? _____

   _____

3. Who gave Janet a fresh carton of milk? _____

   _____

4. Why was Janet happy? _____

   _____

Fill in the blanks with words from the box.

1. A _____ of soap	bottle
2. A _____ of cigarettes	can
3. A _____ of toothpaste	tube
4. A _____ of beans	jar
5. A _____ of bleach	dozen
6. A _____ of chocolates	loaf
7. A _____ of jam	bar
8. A _____ of bread	pack
9. A _____ eggs	pound
10. A _____ of butter	box

Put the words in the box in alphabetical order.

_____

_____

_____

_____

_____

_____

_____

_____

_____

_____

bottle
can
tube
jar
dozen
loaf
bar
pack
pound
box

Use words from the story to complete the following sentences.

1. When the man stood on my foot accidentally, he _____.

2. Mary is a good nurse. She is very _____ every time I see her.

3. The bus driver was angry when I gave him the wrong transfer. I wish he had been more _____.

4. There was a line at the _____ stand when I went to the grocery after work.

Complete the following sentences with the correct form of the words in parentheses.

1. This meat is _____ than that meat. (fresh)

2. These oranges are the _____ in the store. (juicy)

3. Mr. Brown is 93. Mr. Jones is 70. Mr. Brown is _____ than Mr. Jones. (old)

4. John and Mary have four children. Peter is the _____ child. (young)

5. John Paul Getty was the _____ man in the world. (rich)

6. The plane from Los Angeles gets to New York at eleven o'clock AM. The plane from Chicago arrives at one o'clock PM. The Chicago plane arrives two hours _____ than the Los Angeles plane. (late)

Arrange the words in the following sentences in correct order. Write the corrected statement or question.

1. and took out / the milk. / Janet / went / to the refrigerator

   _____

2. was sour. / to find that / surprised / the milk / She was

   _____

3. did / it away? / she throw / Did Janet take / the milk back / or

   _____

4. the milk / you bought / What / was sour? / would you do if

   _____

Finish the following conversation in your own words.

Janet: Excuse me. _____

Check-out clerk: When did_____

Janet: On _____

Check-out clerk: _____

Janet: _____

Fill in the blanks to complete the story. Try not to look back.

Janet had a problem _____ morning. She bought a _____
of milk on Saturday. _____ she opened it this _____,
the milk was sour. _____ took it back to the store. The check-out clerk
_____ and was very friendly. _____ changed the
carton for _____ fresh one. Janet was _____ that the
carton of milk was _____ so quickly. The store _____
and check-out clerk were _____ understanding.

Paying by Check

Vocabulary

graduation   present

jewelry   bracelet

cashier   ID

decides

Mrs. Jones is at Macy's today. She wants to buy a graduation present for her daughter. She decides to go to the jewelry department. The salesperson is very helpful. She shows Mrs. Jones a lot of beautiful necklaces and bracelets. Mrs. Jones chooses a beautiful gold bracelet. She then takes the bracelet to the cashier. Mrs. Jones doesn't have enough cash, so she writes a check. The cashier asks to see her ID. Mrs. Jones shows the cashier her driver's license and her credit card.

Comprehension Questions

1. What does Mrs. Jones want to buy at Macy's? _____

_____

2. Why does she write a check? _____

_____

3. Mrs. Jones gives the cashier a check. What else does the cashier want? _____

_____

4. What does Mrs. Jones show the cashier? _____

_____

Put the words in the box in alphabetical order.

_____

_____

_____

_____

_____

_____

_____

_____

| choose |
| bracelet |
| jewelry |
| driver's |
| cashier |
| necklace |
| graduation |
| takes |
| helpful |

Use words from the story to complete the following sentences.

1. After Mike finishes school, he will have a _____ party.

2. Mrs. Waters can order strawberries or apple pie for dessert. She doesn't know which one to _____ .

3. Margaret _____ to go downtown.

4. If I buy this magazine, I won't have _____ money for the bus fare home.

5. Can I write a _____ for this book?

6. Mei Ling bought a birthday _____ for her mother yesterday.

Rewrite the following sentences.

Example: Mrs. Jones shows the cashier her ID.

   Mrs. Jones shows her ID to the cashier.

1. She buys her daughter a present.

   _____

2. She takes the bracelet to the cashier.

   _____

3. Marion reads her son a story.

   _____

4. Joe wrote his sister a letter.

   _____

5. I made my little boy a cake for this birthday.

   _____

6. Gordon drew a picture for his teacher.

   _____

7. Betty Ann throws John a tennis ball.

   _____

Finish the following conversation in your own words. Use words like *buy, bracelet, enough money, check, ID,* and so on.

Cashier: Good morning. _____

Mrs. Jones: I want _____

Cashier: Will it be on your credit card? _____

Mrs. Jones: No. _____

Cashier: Can I _____

Mrs. Jones: Here is _____

Cashier: _____

Fill in the blanks to complete the story. Try not to look back.

Yesterday Mrs. Jones went _____ town because she wanted _____ buy a graduation present _____ her daughter. She chose _____ gold bracelet. She did _____ have enough money to _____ for it, so she _____ a check. The cashier _____ to see her ID. Mrs. _____ showed the cashier her _____ license and her _____ card.

3 The Old Car

Vocabulary

finish	hospital
together	agree
repair bills	argue
habit	belonged to

John and Linda finish work at five o'clock PM. John picks Linda up from the hospital. They drive home together. Their car is very old. It breaks down sometimes. John wants to sell it, but Linda doesn't. She likes their old car. She says a new car costs too much. John doesn't agree. He says the repair bills for the old car are too high and it uses too much gas. They usually argue about their old car on the way home. It's a habit, because the car belonged to John's grandfather and they both really love it very much.

Comprehension Questions

1. What do John and Linda do after they finish work? _____

_____

2. Why does John want to sell the old car? _____

_____

3. What do they usually do on their way home? _____

_____

4. Why? _____

_____

5. Do *you* think John really wants to sell his grandfather's old car? Why? _____

_____

Circle the letter of the best ending for each sentence to agree with the story.

1. John and Linda
   a. are having dinner.
   b. finish work at five o'clock.
   c. have a baby.
   d. don't go to parties.

2. The old car
   a. goes slowly.
   b. never breaks down.
   c. uses too much gas.
   d. is painted yellow.

3. John's grandfather
   a. lives with John and Linda.
   b. is very rich.
   c. likes repair bills.
   d. used to own the old car.

4. John and Linda

    a. love their old car very much.
b. are buying a washing machine.
c. never argue about their car.
d. have bad habits

Fill in the blanks with words from the box.

1. Smoking is a _____.
2. Politicians _____ about the use of nuclear power.
3. The boys loved *Batman*. They _____ it's a good movie.
4. The plumber sent us a _____ bill.
5. The dog and the kittens play _____ happily.
6. Did you _____ painting the house?

| agree |
| finish |
| habit |
| together |
| repair |
| argue |

Write *true* or *false* at the beginning of each sentence.

_____ 1. John and Linda both finish work at the same time.

_____ 2. John drives home by himself.

_____ 3. Their car breaks down every Tuesday afternoon.

_____ 4. Repair bills for the car are low.

_____ 5. John and Linda have a habit of arguing about their old car.

_____ 6. The car was John's grandfather's.

Rewrite the following sentences.

Example: This scarf belongs to Marianna.

       This is Marianna's scarf.

1. The new house next door belongs to the Lees.

   _____

2. This cat belongs to Jason.

   _____

3. The old car belonged to John's grandfather.

   _____

4. The red coat belongs to me.

   _____

5. That silver brooch belongs to my aunt.

   _____

6. That jacket belongs to Allan.

   _____

Finish the following conversation in your own words. Use words like *sell, costs too much, repair bills,* and so on.

Linda: Hi John.

John :   Hi Linda. Get in. I hope this old car doesn't break down on the way home.

Linda: I hope it doesn't, too. I_____

John: _____

Linda: _____

John: _____

Linda: _____

Fill in the blanks to complete the story. Try not to look back.

John and Linda finish _____ at the same time. _____ picks Linda up from _____ hospital and they drive _____ together. Their car is _____ old. Sometimes it breaks _____. Linda likes their old _____ and doesn't want to _____ it, but John does. _____ says a new car _____ too much. John doesn't _____. He says that the _____ bills for their car _____ too high. He says _____ old car uses too _____ gas. They nearly always _____ about the car on _____ way home. This is _____ habit. They both really _____ their old car, which _____ to John's grandfather.

4 Julie's Job Worries

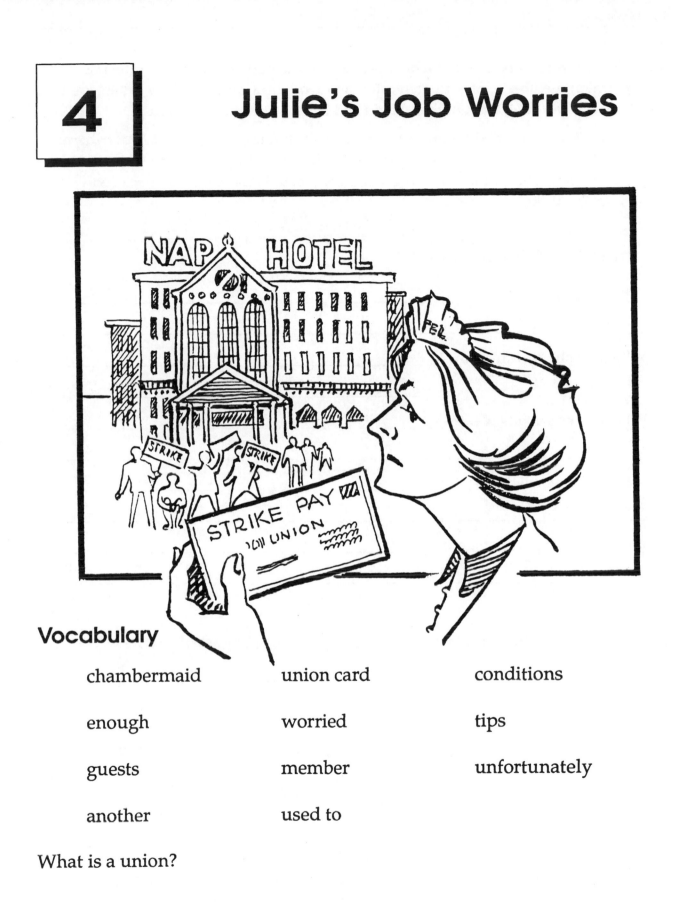

Vocabulary

chambermaid

enough

guests

another

union card

worried

member

used to

conditions

tips

unfortunately

What is a union?

Have you ever been a union member?

Julie is a chambermaid at a big hotel. She has a union card because she is a union member. Unfortunately, she can't work now because the workers are on strike. They want higher wages and better working conditions.

Julie is very worried because the strike might last for a long time. The *strike pay* she gets from the union is not enough to live on. She used to get good tips from the guests at the hotel. She would like to get another job, but all the hotels are closed because of the strike.

Comprehension Questions

1. What is Julie's job? _____

   _____

2. Why isn't she working now? _____

   _____

3. What do the strikers want? _____

   _____

4. Why is she worried? _____

   _____

5. Why can't she get another job? _____

   _____

Write *true* or *false* at the beginning of each sentence.

_____ 1. Julie can't work because she isn't a member of the union.

_____ 2. She used to get good tips from hotel guests.

_____ 3. *Strike pay* is money paid to striking union members by the union.

_____ 4. Julie needs more money to live on.

_____ 5. Some hotels are still open.

_____ 6. Julie's friends tell her that the strike is nearly over.

_____ 7. Members of Julie's union are happy with their working conditions.

Julie is a chambermaid at a big hotel. She has a union card because she is a union member. Unfortunately, she can't work now because the workers are on strike. They want higher wages and better working conditions.

Julie is very worried because the strike might last for a long time. The *strike pay* she gets from the union is not enough to live on. She used to get good tips from the guests at the hotel. She would like to get another job, but all the hotels are closed because of the strike.

Comprehension Questions

1. What is Julie's job? _____
_____

2. Why isn't she working now? _____
_____

3. What do the strikers want? _____
_____

4. Why is she worried? _____
_____

5. Why can't she get another job? _____
_____

Write *true* or *false* at the beginning of each sentence.

_____ 1. Julie can't work because she isn't a member of the union.

_____ 2. She used to get good tips from hotel guests.

_____ 3. *Strike pay* is money paid to striking union members by the union.

_____ 4. Julie needs more money to live on.

_____ 5. Some hotels are still open.

_____ 6. Julie's friends tell her that the strike is nearly over.

_____ 7. Members of Julie's union are happy with their working conditions.

4 Julie's Job Worries

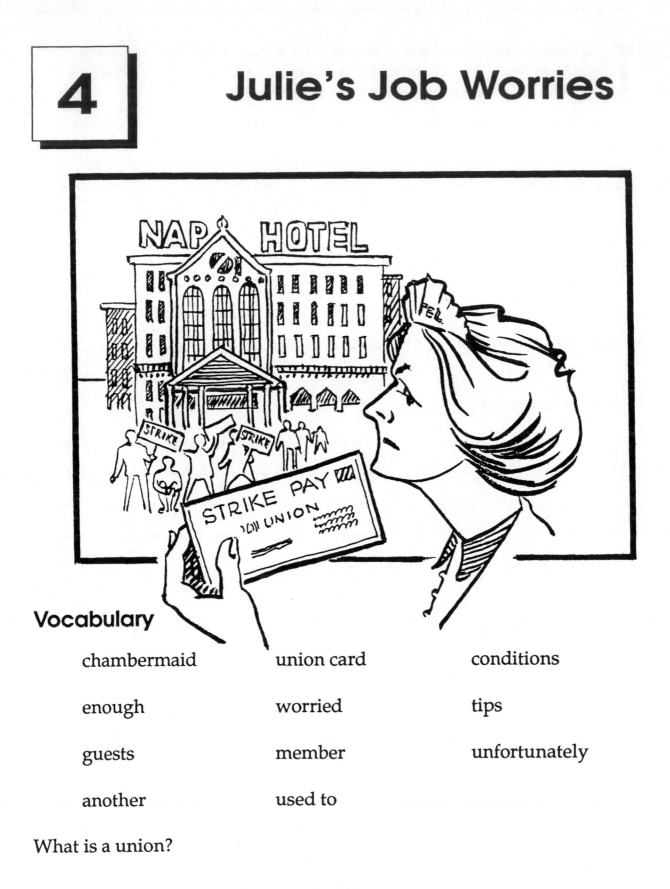

Vocabulary

chambermaid	union card	conditions
enough	worried	tips
guests	member	unfortunately
another	used to	

What is a union?

Have you ever been a union member?

Fill in the blank with the letter of the definition that best matches each word.

_____ 1. A chambermaid   a. stays in a hotel.

_____ 2. A member   b. works in an office.

_____ 3. A guest   c. helps you plan a trip.

_____ 4. A waitress   d. makes beds and cleans hotel rooms.

_____ 5. A secretary   e. works in a restaurant.

_____ 6. A travel agent   f. belongs to a group.

Use words from the story to complete the following sentences.

1. Sally has broken her leg. _____ she won't be able to ski in the race next month.

2. The working _____ at the restaurant are very good.

3. I don't understand this book, and I am _____ that I might fail the test.

4. This string is not long _____ to tie around my parcel.

5. When Jane was little, she _____ to eat a lot of candy.

6. Sandra dropped her ice-cream cone on the sidewalk, and now she wants _____ another one.

Finish these sentences.

1. Julie can't work because _____

_____

2. Julie is worried _____

_____

3. She has a union card _____

_____

4. The hotels are closed _____

_____

5. Tai Cheng's dog is barking_____

_____

6. Susan is going downtown _____

_____

Choose a word in column A and a word in column B to make a new compound word. Write the correct words in the blanks.

1. all the news in it

   _____

2. she works in a hotel

   _____

3. the teacher writes on it

   _____

4. you sit in it

   _____

5. not complete

   _____

A	B
arm	board
chalk	way
news	maid
half	paper
chamber	chair

Fill in the blanks to complete the story. Try not to look back.

Julie is a chambermaid. _____ used to work at _____ big hotel, but now _____ union workers are on _____. Julie is a union _____ and has a union _____. Because of the strike, _____ cannot work.

She is _____ because her friends say _____ the strike might last _____ a long time. Her *strike pay* _____ not enough for her _____ live on. In her _____ job she got good _____ from the hotel guests. _____ wants to find another _____, but the strike has _____ all the hotels.

Chinese New Year

Vocabulary

paste	luck	special
nobody	allowed	reunion
relatives	packets	visit
delicious	firecrackers	

Is New Year's Day an important holiday in your native country?

What is the most important holiday in your country?

Tomorrow is New Year's Day. Mei Ling is very excited. Today, she's helping her sisters clean the house. Her father is pasting red paper on the front door for good luck. Her mother is in the kitchen baking special Chinese New Year cookies. Everybody is doing something because nobody is allowed to work on New Year's Day. Usually there is a big reunion dinner with all the relatives on New Year's Eve.

On New Year's Day, Mei Ling and her sisters always put on new clothes. They kiss their parents and wish them Happy New Year. Their parents give them red packets of lucky money. Then they visit friends and relatives. All Chinese children love Chinese New Year because there are delicious things to eat, firecrackers to play with, new clothes, and lucky money. They also love Chinese New Year because it lasts for fifteen days.

Comprehension Questions

1. Why are Mei Ling and her sisters cleaning the house? _____

   _____

2. When is there usually a reunion dinner with all the relatives? _____

   _____

3. What do Mei Ling and her sisters do on New Year's Day? _____

   _____

4. What do their parents give them? _____

   _____

5. Why do the children love Chinese New Year? _____

   _____

6. What color do the Chinese use for good luck? _____

   _____

Circle the letter of the best ending for each sentence to agree with the story.

1. Mei Ling is
   a. pasting red paper on the front door.
   b. baking special Chinese New Year cookies.
   c helping her sisters clean the house.
   d. eating a big reunion dinner.

2. Mei Ling's mother
   a. is wearing new clothes.
   b. is eating delicious things.
   c. is baking special Chinese New Year cookies.
   d. is helping the children clean the house.

3. All Chinese children
   a. paste red paper on Mei Ling's front door.
   b. love Chinese New Year.
   c. have a reunion on New Year's Day.
   d. work on New Year's Day.

4. Chinese New Year
   a. is always on October 17.
   b. lasts for two days.
   c. is a time when everyone works.
   d. lasts for fifteen days.

Fill in the blanks in this paragraph using the words *nothing* or *nobody.*

I went to Jacob's house and _____ was home. There was _____ to do, so I went home. All my friends were on vacation. I had _____ to talk to. I was bored because there was _____ to do. So I went to a movie. It wasn't a good movie. _____ sat beside me. I reached in my pocket for money to buy popcorn. I had _____ in my pocket, not even my driver's license. There was _____ I could borrow money from, so I had _____ to eat at the show. When the movie was over, I went home. There was _____ good on TV, so I went to bed.

Fill in the blanks with the letter of the definition that best matches each word.

____ 1. pasted   a. good to eat
____ 2. good luck   b. not a single person
____ 3. special   c. makes good things happen
____ 4. nobody   d. stuck
____ 5. allowed   e. not ordinary
____ 6. delicious   f. let, permitted

Finish the following conversation using words from the vocabulary.

Mei Ling: Hi Dad. Why are you pasting the paper on the door?

Father: _____

What are you and your sisters doing?

Mei Ling: _____

Father: What is your mother doing? _____

Mei Ling: _____

Father: You children all like Chinese New Year, don't you?

Mei Ling: _____

Fill in the blanks to complete the story. Try not to look back.

Mei Ling is excited _____ tomorrow is New Year's _____.
Today she is helping _____ sisters clean the house.
_____ father is pasting red _____ on the front door
_____ good luck. Her mother _____ in the kitchen
baking _____ Chinese New Year cookies. _____ is
doing something because _____ is allowed to work
_____ New Year's Day. Usually _____ is a reunion
dinner _____ New Year's Eve with _____ the relatives.

On New _____ Day Mei Ling and _____ sisters
always put on _____ clothes. They kiss their _____
and wish them Happy _____ Year. Their parents give
_____ red packets of lucky _____. Then they visit
friends _____ relatives. All Chinese children _____
Chinese New Year because _____ are delicious things to
_____. There are also firecrackers, _____ clothes, and
lucky money. _____ also love Chinese New Year because it lasts for
_____ days.

The Lost Child

Vocabulary

department store   half-price

sale   corduroy

nylon   busy

forgot

Have you ever lost one of your children? Where?

29

Alice Lau is married and has four children. Three of them are at school. The youngest is three years old. His name is Bobby. This afternoon, Alice and Bobby went downtown. There was a sale at one of the big department stores. Children's clothes were half-price. Alice bought some red corduroy pants for her daughter. She bought a green nylon jacket for her oldest son. She was very busy and forgot about Bobby. When she looked for him, he was gone!

Comprehension Questions

1. How many children does Alice have? _____

    _____

2. What does Alice do during the day? _____

    _____

3. How many children are at home during the day? _____

    _____

4. Where was the sale in children's clothes? _____

    _____

5. What did Alice buy her oldest son? _____

    _____

6. What do *you* think happened to Bobby? _____

    _____

Complete the following sentences with the correct form of the words in parentheses.

1. The green jacket looked _____ than any of the others. (nice)

2. It was _____ than the black one. (cheap)

3. Wai Ping is _____ than her sister. (tall)

4. The weather in New York is _____ than in California. (cold)

5. Do you have a pencil that is _____ than this one? (sharp)

6. This book is _____ to read than the one I read last week. (easy)

Make new compound words by choosing words from the box to fill in the blanks.

1. down _____
2. half- _____
3. baby _____
4. neck _____
5. country _____
6. for _____
7. school _____

lace
price
age
got
town
sitter
side

Complete these sentences with a word from column A and a word from column B.

1. Linda bought a _____ skirt to wear on the first day of school.
2. Mary has a _____ evening dress.
3. Jack wants a _____ winter coat.
4. Tom needs a _____ workshirt.
5. Mary's children have _____ ski jackets for Seattle's rainy weather.
6. Do you like my new _____ pants?

A	B
red	polyester
blue	silk
green	cotton
yellow	corduroy
black	nylon
purple	wool

Use words from the vocabulary to fill in the blanks.

1. I _____ to take the books back to the library.
2. The _____ stores are all open on Friday nights until nine o'clock.
3. _____ is a material with lines, or ridges, in it.
4. Alice is _____ making cookies for Halloween.
5. When will these shirts be on _____?

Finish the following conversation in your own words.

Alice: These pants are size 8. Do you have any size 10s?

Clerk: _____

Alice: Okay. I'll take them. Do you have_____

Clerk: Yes. _____

Alice: I need a jacket _____

Clerk: _____

Alice: How _____

Clerk: They are $ _____

Fill in the blanks to complete the story. Try not to look back.

Alice Lau is _____. She has four children. _____ of
them are at _____. The youngest is three _____ old.
His name is Bobby. This afternoon Alice and _____ went downtown.
There was _____ sale at one of _____ big department
stores. Children's _____ were half-price. Alice bought _____
red corduroy pants for _____ daughter and a green _____
jacket for her oldest _____. She was very busy _____
forgot about Bobby. _____ she looked for him, _____
was gone.

7 Bobby's Adventure

Vocabulary

adventure   cashier

describes   voice

cross   hug

public address system

What would you do if you lost one of your children?

How would you feel when the child was found?

Alice Lau's son Bobby is lost in the department store. Alice goes to the cashier and tells her that Bobby is lost. The cashier is very kind and tells Alice not to worry. Then she asks Alice what Bobby looks like. Alice describes him to the cashier.

Suddenly Alice hears the cashier's voice on the public address system in the store. "A little boy is lost in the store. He is small, has black hair, and is wearing brown pants and a blue jacket. If you find him, please bring him to the children's department."

In a few minutes a kind lady comes to the children's department. Bobby is holding her hand. "I found him at the candy counter," she says to Alice. Alice thanks the lady. Alice isn't cross with Bobby, and she gives him a little hug.

Comprehension Questions

1. What does Alice do when she finds that Bobby is lost? _____

   _____

2. What does the cashier ask Alice? _____

   _____

3. What words does Alice hear on the public address system? _____

   _____

4. What does Bobby look like? _____

   _____

5. Who brings Bobby back? _____

   _____

6. Where was he? _____

   _____

7. Put the answers to questions 5 and 6 into one sentence. _____

   _____

Circle the letter of the best ending for each sentence to agree with the story.

1. The cashier
   a. doesn't listen to Alice.
   b. tells her not to worry.
   c. is rude.
   d. gives Alice some money.

2. Bobby is
   a. seven years old.
   b. a boy with blonde hair.
   c. wearing a blue jacket.
   d. crying.

3. A lady
   a. is at the laundromat.
   b. complains to the cashier.
   c. finds Bobby at the candy counter.
   d. is cross.

4. Alice
   a. is crying.
   b. buys a green sweater.
   c. is at the candy counter.
   d. gives Bobby a hug.

Fill in the blanks with words from the box.

1. Macy's is a large _____ store.

2. The children all wear _____ in the winter.

3. The waitress is standing behind the _____.

4. Can you _____ your new house to me?

5. Stan had an exciting _____ yesterday.

6. Mrs. Wilson got very _____ because the dog ate all the birthday cake.

describe
cross
adventure
counter
jackets
department

Finish the following conversation in your own words.

Cashier: What is the matter, madam? Can I help you?

Alice: _____

Cashier: What does he look like?

Alice: _____

Cashier: I will give his description over the public address system in the store, and someone will bring him back.

FIVE MINUTES LATER

Lady: _____

Alice: _____

✳The following words all start with the same letter. Put them in alphabetical order by looking at the second letter in each word.

store   sell   _____   _____
small   space   _____   _____
summer   Sam   _____   _____
shoes   sneeze   _____   _____
son   singing   _____   _____
system   school   _____   _____

Fill in the blanks to complete the story. Try not to look back.

Bobby is lost. His _____, Alice Lau, goes to _____ cashier and tells her _____ Bobby is lost. The _____ is kind and tells _____ not to worry. She _____ Alice what Bobby looks _____.

The cashier speaks into _____ public address system. "A _____ boy is lost. He _____ small and has black _____. He is wearing a _____ jacket and brown pants. _____ bring him to the _____ department if you _____ him."

In a few _____ a kind lady _____ to the children's _____. Bobby is holding her _____. "I found him at _____ candy counter," she says _____ Alice. Alice thanks the _____. Then she gives Bobby a _____ hug.

8 House Hunting

Vocabulary

carpenter	rent
colorful	story
old-fashioned	workroom

flower beds

How did you find your house or apartment?

Mr. and Mrs. Black are looking for a house because they are tired of living in their small apartment. Mrs. Black would like to have more room for her large family. She would also like a garden of her own. Mr. Black wants a room for his carpenter's tools.

Every morning, Mr. Black reads the "House for Rent" ads in the newspaper. His wife walks around the streets and looks for "For Rent" signs. Last week, she found a lovely house for rent. It is an old, green wooden house. It has two stories, a basement, and beautiful old-fashioned windows. There are many old oak trees and colorful flower beds in the garden.

Mrs. Black knocks on the door and a woman answers. She asks Mrs. Black to come inside. The rooms are very neat and clean. There is a workroom in the basement. When Mrs. Black gets home, she phones the owner.

Comprehension Questions

1. Why are the Blacks looking for a house? _____

   _____

2. Mrs. Black sees a house for rent. What is it like? _____

   _____

3. What is in the garden of the house? _____

   _____

4. What can Mr. Black put in the workroom in the basement? _____

   _____

5. Does Mrs. Black decide that she wants to rent the house? How do you know? _____

   _____

Complete the following sentences with the correct form of the words in parentheses.

1. Today I am _____ to town. (go)

2. I am _____ for a pair of shoes. (shop)

3. Anna is _____ her grandmother. (telephone)

4. Quick! The pancakes are _____. (burn)

5. The picnic is canceled because Grant's mother is _____ sick. (feel)

6. I am _____ to write a story. (try)

Use words from the vocabulary to fill in the blanks.

1. The rented house was built in 1920 and is more _____ than the new one across the street.

2. Anna's red blouse and yellow skirt are very _____.

3. Jane's father is a _____. He is building a house in his spare time.

4. La Hing has a _____ in the basement of her house.

5. Gretchen's uncle hasn't got enough money to buy a house, so he is going to _____ one.

Arrange the words in each sentence in the correct order.

1. in his workroom. / keeps / and nails / Mr. Black / hammers, screwdrivers,

_____

2. you tell if / the house down the street / How can / is for rent?

_____

3. an old, / carpet / bought / secondhand / Mrs. Brown / red / for the living room.

_____

Write down Mrs. Black's conversation with the owner of the house. Ask

- about the rent
- whether there is a refrigerator and stove
- if he minds pets or children
- when the Blacks can move in if they rent it

Mrs. Black: _____

_____

Owner: _____

_____

Mrs. Black: _____

_____

Owner: _____

_____

Mrs. Black: _____

_____

Owner: _____

_____

Mrs. Black: _____

_____

Owner: _____

_____

Fill in the blanks to complete the story. Try not to look back.

Mr. and Mrs. Black _____ tired of living in _____ small apartment. They are _____ for a house to _____. Mrs. Black wants more _____ for her large family. _____ also wants a garden. _____ Black wants a room _____ his carpentry.

Mr. Black _____ all the "House for _____" ads in the newspaper. _____ Black walks around the _____ looking for "For Rent" _____. One day she sees _____ lovely house with _____ in front. The house _____ old. It has two _____ and beautiful old-fashioned _____. It is made of _____ and is painted green. _____ is a garden with _____ oak trees and colorful _____.

Mrs. Black knocks on _____ door. A woman answers _____ asks her to come _____. The rooms are neat _____ clean. There is a _____ in the basement. Mrs. _____ is very excited. As _____ as she gets home, _____ phones the owner.

9

The Christmas Party

Vocabulary

girlfriend	manager
noisy	midnight
taxi	

Do you know anyone who has been stopped for drinking and driving?
What happened?

Tam and his girlfriend went to a Christmas party on Saturday night. Tam's girlfriend works in an office. She is an office manager. It was the office party. They all had a good time. Some people danced. Some talked to friends. Some sang songs. Everybody ate and drank. Some people drank too much, and they were very noisy. At midnight, Tam said, "Police stop a lot of cars at Christmas time. Don't drink and drive. Take a taxi."

Comprehension Questions

1. What night was the office party? _____

   _____

2. Who did Tam go to the party with? _____

   _____

3. What is Tam's girlfriend's job? _____

   _____

4. Some people at the party drank too much. What did Tam say to them? _____

   _____

5. How do the police stop cars at Christmas time? _____

   _____

Choose a word from column A and a word from column B to make a new compound word. Write the correct words in the blanks.

1. The plane will land at the _____.

2. After _____, Tam goes to work.

3. His _____ works in an office.

4. _____ is coming to the party.

5. If you drink, don't drive! Remember, there are _____!

6. Tam's boss has a _____ today.

A	B
every	blocks
break	one
hang	fast
air	friend
girl	port
road	over

Two words are underlined in each sentence. Cross out the wrong one.

1. <u>Before</u> / <u>often</u> I went to work, I had breakfast.

2. In the winter we <u>never</u> / <u>ever</u> have dinner at the beach.

3. If you <u>drink</u> / <u>eat</u> too much, you will probably get drunk.

4. Jim is going to <u>marry</u> / <u>merry</u> an office manager.

5. Let's take a <u>wheel</u> / <u>taxi</u> to the airport. I don't want to wait for the bus.

Complete the following sentences.

1. I have a cut on my hand. I cut _____ with a knife.

2. They went home from the party by _____.

3. My mother and I were home by _____.

4. You will have to stay by _____ if I can't get your uncle to come over.

5. She is going to knit _____ a new sweater.

6. We went to a movie on Saturday by _____.

Fill in the blanks with words from the box.

1. Yesterday I was late, but today I got _____ early.

2. We got _____ on June 20, 1976.

3. Myrna got _____ for her hair.

4. I get _____ a month at my job.

5. Will you get _____ for me?

6. Maria got _____ when her husband didn't come home from work.

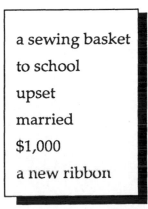

a sewing basket

to school

upset

married

$1,000

a new ribbon

Unscramble the words in the box and put the correct word and its letter in the blanks.

Example: The office party was on ___Saturday___ night.

1. It was a Christmas _____.

2. Tam's girlfriend is an office _____.

3. Some people _____ too much.

4. They were very _____.

5. The _____ stop a lot of cars at Christmas.

6. It is a good idea to take a _____.

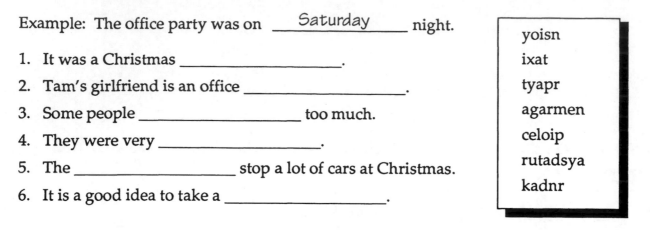

yoisn

ixat

tyapr

agarmen

celoip

rutadsya

kadnr

Fill in the blanks to complete the story. Try not to look back.

Tam's girlfriend is an _____ manager. On Saturday night _____ and Tam went to _____ office party. It was _____ Christmas party. There were _____ lot of people at _____ party. They all had _____ good time eating and _____. They danced and sang _____. Some people had too much _____ drink. They were very _____. Tam said, "Police stop _____ lot of cars at _____ time. Don't drink and _____. Take a taxi."

10

Mr. Specogna's Success

Vocabulary

logger	machines
check	still
spare	look for
paid for	explain

Have you ever found or won anything valuable? What did you do?

What would you do if you won $1,000,000?

Mr. Specogna came to California forty-two years ago. He came with his family from Italy. He went to the northern part of California to work as a logger. He cut down very tall trees. Forty years ago, he bought a book for fifty cents. The book explained how to look for gold. His wife and family helped him.

In the 1960s, he found some gold on his land. He asked a big company to check this gold. They used big machines, and they found a lot of gold on his land. This year, the company paid Mr. Specogna about $500,000 for his land. Now he is a rich man, but he still works as a logger. He still looks for gold in his spare time.

Comprehension Questions

1. When Mr. Specogna came from Italy, where did he go? _____

   _____

2. What did he do? _____

   _____

3. How did he learn to find gold? _____

   _____

4. What did he do when he found gold in the 1960s? _____

   _____

5. How much money did Mr. Specogna get paid for his land? _____

   _____

6. Mr. Specogna is very rich. What does he do now? _____

   _____

Fill in the blanks with words from the box.

1. He decided _____ work as a logger.
2. She paid seventy-five cents _____ an ice-cream cone.
3. Mr. Specogna worked _____ the north when he came from Italy.
4. There were flowers growing _____ the road.
5. There is someone _____ the door.

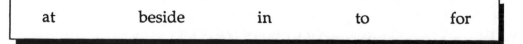

| at | beside | in | to | for |

Make the following groups of words into sentences.

Example: Mr. Specogna / forty-two years ago

Mr. Specogna came to California forty-two years ago.

1. Mr. Specogna / his wife and family _____

_____

2. book / fifty cents _____

_____

3. logger / northern California _____

_____

4. big company / $500,000 _____

_____

5. rich man / logger _____

_____

Put the words from the box in alphabetical order.

_____   _____

_____   _____

_____   _____

_____   _____

_____   _____

still	helped
tall	north
came	bought
big	found
forty	family

Number the following sentences in order. Which happened first, second, and so on?

____ Mr. Specogna asked a big company to check his gold.

____ Mr. Specogna bought a book for fifty cents.

____ Mr. Specogna is very rich now.

____ Mr. Specogna came from Italy forty-two years ago.

____ Mr. Specogna still works as a logger.

____ He cut down very tall trees in northern California.

____ In the 1960s Mr. Specogna found some gold.

Use the words in the box to complete these sentences.

1. Seafood makes Eric sick, so he _____ eats it.
2. We don't go to restaurants. But _____ on someone's birthday, Dad takes us to a special place to eat.
3. Did you _____ win any money in the lottery?
4. I _____ go to bed early, but not all the time.
5. Macy's is _____ open on Friday nights.

usually
ever
never
always
sometimes

Fill in the blanks with words from the box.

1. Jim is working as a _____ this summer.
2. Do you have any _____ ribbon left over?
3. I will _____ my grocery list to see if I have remembered everything.
4. The men who work at the park use big _____ to cut the lawns.
5. Mr. Jones retired last year, but he _____ goes to his office every Friday.

still
logger
check
machines
spare

Fill in the blanks to complete the story. Try not to look back.

Forty-two years ago, Mr. _____ came to California from _____. He worked as a _____. Forty years ago he _____ a book for fifty _____. The book explained how _____ look for gold. His _____ and family _____ him.

In the 1960s, _____ Specogna found gold on his _____. He asked _____ big company to check the _____. They used machines and _____ a lot of gold _____ his property. This year _____ paid him about $500,000 _____ his land. Now he _____ rich. He still works _____ a logger and looks _____ gold in his spare _____.

Mrs. Wong's Visit to the Laundromat

Vocabulary

laundromat	laundry
broken	instructions
soapsuds	shocked
careful	upset

Mrs. Wong was doing her laundry today, when her washing machine broke down. So, she took her dirty clothes to the laundromat. She put the clothes into the washer, but she didn't have enough quarters. She asked a lady for change.

She said, "Excuse me. Do you have change for a dollar?"

Mrs. Wong was in a hurry because she wanted to go downtown. She didn't read the instructions. The instructions said: USE ONE CUP OF SOAP POWDER ONLY. Mrs. Wong put two cups in. In ten minutes, there were soapsuds all over the place. Mrs. Wong was shocked and upset. Next time she will be more careful!

Comprehension Questions

1. Why didn't Mrs. Wong do her laundry at home? _____

_____

2. What did she do with her dirty clothes? _____

_____

3. Why didn't she read the instructions? _____

_____

4. What happened? _____

_____

5. What lesson did Mrs. Wong learn? _____

_____

Fill in the blanks with the letter of the definition that best matches each word.

_____ 1. instructions   a. polite way to begin a question

_____ 2. laundromat   b. quarters, dimes, and nickels

_____ 3. change   c. sentences that tell how to operate a machine

_____ 4. broken down   d. unpleasantly surprised

_____ 5. shocked   e. place where there are a lot of washing machines

_____ 6. excuse me   f. not working

Put the following words in alphabetical order.

instructions   _____

laundromat   _____

change   _____

broken down   _____

shocked   _____

excuse me   _____

Make each sentence into a question using the words *when, where,* or *how much.*

Example: This soap costs eighty-five cents.

How much does this soap cost?

1. The plumber will come on Wednesday morning.

_____

2. The tickets for the movie are three dollars each.

_____

3. I found this puppy at the end of the lane.

_____

4. Elli is going home in an hour.

_____

5. The police station is around the corner.

_____

6. The lady in the green hat is buying six yards of material.

_____

Finish the following conversation in your own words.

Mrs. Wong: Good morning. _____

Lady: Yes, I do. Do you want quarters?

Mrs. Wong: Yes, please. How many _____

Lady: Two. Put in two quarters to do your laundry.

Mrs. Wong: _____

Cross out the wrong word in the parentheses.

1. She doesn't have (enough, less) wool to finish her sweater.
2. It is late, and Mrs. Wong is in a (quickly, hurry).
3. Ida put the (wet, raining) clothes in the dryer.
4. Do you have (difference, change) for a dollar?
5. Mrs. Wong put (too much, too many) soap in the washing machine.
6. She went to town to buy some new (cloths, clothes) for the children to wear to school.

Fill in the blanks to complete the story. Try not to look back.

Mrs. Wong's washing machine _____ down, so she _____
to the laundromat to _____ her laundry. She put _____
dirty clothes into the _____. She didn't have enough _____.
She asked a lady _____ change.

Mrs. Wong was _____ a hurry because she _____
to go downtown. She _____ read the instructions carefully.
_____ put in two cups _____ soap instead of only
_____. In ten minutes there _____ soapsuds all over
the _____. Mrs. Wong was shocked _____ upset. Next
time she _____ be more careful.

 **12**

All He Wanted Was a Glass of Water

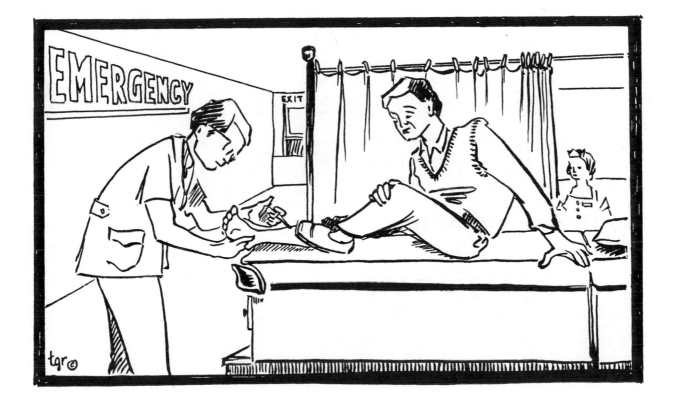

Vocabulary

woke	thirsty	unfortunately
emergency room	a shot	stitches
sole	badly	probably

Have you ever gone to an emergency room? Where? Why?

53

Franz woke up in the middle of the night because he was thirsty. He went downstairs to get a glass of water. Unfortunately, he dropped the glass on the floor. Because it was dark, Franz couldn't see and he stepped on the broken glass. He had to go to the emergency room of the hospital because his foot was bleeding badly. The doctor gave Franz a shot and put four stitches in the sole of his foot.

Today Franz is having trouble walking because his foot is sore. He'll probably go to see his family doctor this afternoon.

Comprehension Questions

1. When did Franz cut his foot? _____

_____

2. Why did he go downstairs? _____

_____

3. What did he do after he cut his foot? _____

_____

4. What happened at the hospital? _____

_____

5. Why is it hard for Franz to walk today? _____

_____

6. What will he probably do this afternoon? _____

_____

Number the following sentences in order. Which happened first, second, and so on?

____ Franz went to the emergency room.

____ The doctor gave Franz a shot.

____ The doctor put four stitches in Franz's foot.

____ Franz will probably go to see his family doctor this afternoon.

____ Franz woke up in the middle of the night.

____ Today his foot is sore.

____ Franz dropped a glass on the floor.

____ Franz cut his foot.

Use words from the box to complete the following sentences.

1. In the middle of the night Franz went _____.

2. He dropped a glass of water _____.

3. His foot was bleeding, so Franz went _____.

4. The doctor put four stitches _____.

5. The emergency room is _____.

6. Today Franz will probably go _____.

at the hospital	downstairs
to see his family doctor	in his foot
on the floor	to the emergency room

Choose words from the box that mean the same thing as the underlined words. Rewrite the sentence.

1. The bottom of my foot is sore.

   _____

2. I have a cut on the inside of my hand.

   _____

3. The doctor gave me a needle in my arm.

   _____

4. He also sewed up the cut on my leg.

   _____

5. It was bad luck that John was fired.

   _____

6. In hot weather I want to drink water.

   _____

7. I stopped sleeping when the alarm clock rang.

   _____

unfortunately	put stitches in
shot	am thirsty
my palm	sole
woke up	

Franz phones his family doctor to make an appointment. Write down the conversation between Franz and the nurse who answers the phone.

_____

_____

_____

_____

_____

_____

Fill in the blanks with words from the box.

1. the _____ of my foot
2. the _____ of my house
3. the _____ of her hand
4. the _____ of the company
5. the _____ of the hospital
6. the _____ of the night

a. middle
b. roof
c. president
d. sole
e. emergency room
f. palm

Fill in the blanks to complete the story. Try not to look back.

Franz woke up in _____ middle of the night. _____ was thirsty, so he _____ downstairs to get a _____ of water. Unfortunately, he _____ the glass on the _____. He stepped on some _____ glass and cut his _____. Because his foot was _____ badly, he went to _____ emergency room at the _____. The doctor gave him _____ shot and put four _____ in the sole of _____ foot.

Today Franz is _____ trouble walking because his _____ is sore. He'll probably go _____ see his family doctor _____ afternoon.

13 Change of Address

Vocabulary

neighborhood	postal clerk
fireplace	associates
medium	story

Have you ever moved to a new house or apartment in the United States?

How did you get your mail delivered to your new house?

The Jacksons bought a new house last month. It is a two-story house in a quiet neighborhood. There is a small front yard and a medium-sized backyard. There is a fireplace in the living room and a garage beside the house. The Jacksons are going to move into their new house soon.

Yesterday, Mr. Jackson was at the Post Office. He wanted a change-of-address kit. He needs to mail change-of-address cards to his friends and his business associates. He also gave a change-of-address card to the postal clerk. Now the Post Office will change the address on his mail for the next twelve months.

Comprehension Questions

1. What is in the living room of the Jacksons' new house? _____

   _____

2. What does Mr. Jackson want at the Post Office?_____

   _____

3. Who will Mr. Jackson send his change-of-address cards to? _____

   _____

4. How long will the Post Office change the address on Mr. Jackson's mail? _____

   _____

Use words from the story to complete the following sentences.

1. Most houses in the _____ are the same as the Jacksons' house.

2. They are happy to have a _____ for their car.

3. These lemons are too small, and those lemons are too big. Do you have some that are _____-sized?

4. Mr. Jackson has lunch with his business _____ every Tuesday.

Use the words in the box to complete the following sentences.

1. It is July. We are going ~~go~~ (to) on vacation in August. We are going to go on vacation _____ month.

2. It is February. Christmas was two months _____.

3. It is November. In October we bought a car. We bought a car _____ month.

4. It is August. School starts in September. School starts _____ a month.

next
ago
last
in

Complete the following sentences with the correct form of the words in parentheses.

1. The Jacksons will be _____ to the bus stop when they move into their new house than they are now. (close)

2. Mr. Jackson's backyard is _____ than the front yard. (big)

3. Some stamps are _____ than others. (cheap)

4. He is a very busy man. He is _____ than his associates. (busy)

5. The little girl bought the _____ ice-cream cone in the store. (large)

Rewrite the second paragraph of the story, beginning with *Tomorrow Mr. Jackson will go to the Post Office.*

_____

_____

_____

_____

_____

_____

_____

Finish the following conversation in your own words.

Postal Clerk: When are you moving?

Mr. Jackson: _____

Postal Clerk: You need a _____

Mr. Jackson: _____

Postal Clerk: _____

Mr. Jackson: Will the Post Office _____

Postal Clerk: Yes, for the next twelve months. _____

Mr. Jackson: _____

Fill in the blanks to complete the story. Try not to look back.

The Jacksons bought a _____ house last month. It is _____ two-story house _____ a quiet neighborhood. There _____ a fireplace in the _____ room and a garage _____ the house. The Jacksons _____ going to move into _____ new house soon.

Yesterday, Mr. _____ was at the Post Office. He _____ a change-_____ -address kit. He needs _____ for his friends and _____ business associates. The postal _____ also gave him a _____ card for the post _____ . Now the _____ Office will change the _____ on all his mail _____ the next twelve months.

14 Blood Donors

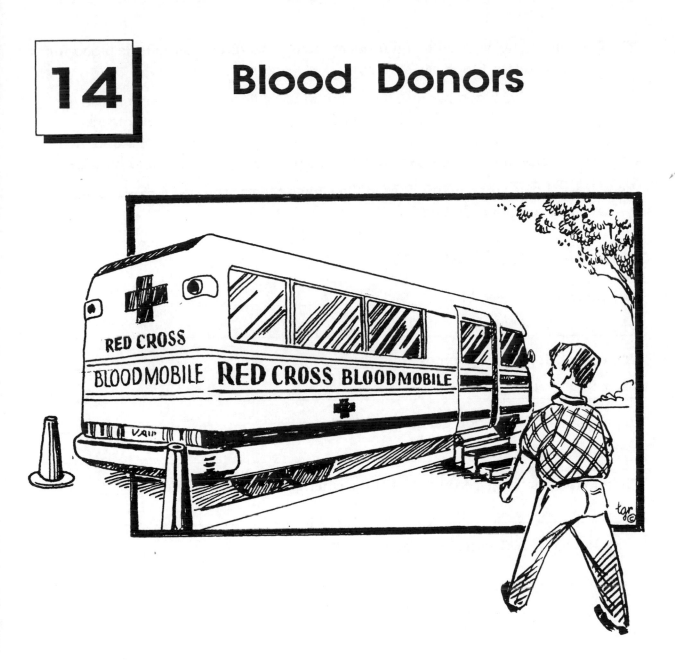

Vocabulary

donor	operations
collects	pint
volunteers	clinic

Have you ever been a blood donor?

What is your blood type?

H ospitals always need blood for operations. The Red Cross collects blood for the hospitals. Blood can save lives.

People give blood because they want to help. They want to save lives. We call these people blood donors. Blood donors don't get paid. They are volunteers. People give blood at Red Cross clinics. At the clinic a nurse takes a pint of blood. It doesn't hurt. After you give blood, the Red Cross gives you free drinks and cookies.

Red Cross clinics are in many cities in the United States. The Red Cross nurses are always happy to see blood donors.

Comprehension Questions

1. Why do hospitals need blood? _____

_____

2. Who collects it for the hospitals? _____

_____

3. Do people who give blood get money for it? _____

_____

4. What do the nurses give volunteers at the clinic after they give blood? _____

_____

5. What do you do if you decide to give blood? _____

_____

6. Where can you give blood in your city? _____

_____

Use words from the vocabulary to complete the following sentences.

1. A _____ of milk is too much to feed the cats.
2. Joanna takes her two-month-old son to the well-baby _____ every Tuesday.
3. Mrs. McGreer has had three _____ since last summer!
4. The _____ at the library are very helpful. They work there once a week and don't get paid.
5. Joan's little girl _____ pink shells that she finds at the beach.

Write down the telephone conversation between you and the nurse at the Red Cross clinic. Ask her where you go to give blood, what time the clinic is open, and so on.

_____

_____

_____

_____

_____

_____

_____

_____

_____

Fill in the blanks to complete the story. Try not to look back.

All hospitals use a _____ of blood for operations. _____ Red Cross collects it _____ the hospitals. People give _____ to the Red Cross. _____ are called volunteers because _____ don't get paid for _____ . When someone wants to _____ blood, he goes to _____ Red Cross clinic. There _____ nurse takes a pint _____ blood. After you give _____ , you are given free _____ and cookies.

Red Cross clinics _____ in many cities in _____ United States. If you want to _____ blood, just go to _____ of them. They are _____ happy to see blood _____ .

Fill in each blank with the correct word from the parentheses.

1. Our house is _____ the Red Cross clinic. (in, near)

2. The nurse takes blood _____ volunteers. (above, from)

3. She puts the cookies _____ the table. (in, on)

4. She puts the drinks _____ them. (beside, under)

5. Will you give _____ blood to the Red Cross? (some, many)

6. Adam is standing _____ the table. (back, behind)

Write *true* or *false* at the beginning of each sentence.

_____ 1. Hospitals need blood for operations.

_____ 2. The Red Cross pays five dollars a pint for blood.

_____ 3. If you want to give blood, you should go to the hospital.

_____ 4. Blood donors are people who give blood.

_____ 5. The nurse at the clinic gives the donors something to drink.

Find the meaning for each word and circle the letter.

1. volunteers
   - a. people who don't get paid for work
   - b. circus performers
   - c. paid workers

2. collects
   - a. part of a shirt
   - b. a volunteer
   - c. gathers

3. decides
   - a. draws
   - b. makes up his mind
   - c. goes by bus

Mr. McIver's Revenge

Vocabulary

revenge   appliance

customers   deposit

insufficient funds   court

How do you pay for things you buy?

Do you ever write checks?

M r. McIver owns an appliance store. Last month he lost more than $10,000. Customers bought appliances from him and paid by check. He deposited the checks in the bank, but they came back marked *insufficient funds*.

When he asked the police for help, they couldn't help him. It takes a long time and a lot of money to go to court. Mr. McIver had a good idea. He put a big sign in front of his store. On the sign he wrote the names of the customers with bad checks. Everyone can read the names of his bad customers. No one has given him a bad check since he put up the sign.

Comprehension Questions

1. How much money did Mr. McIver lose last month? _____

_____

2. What happened after he deposited his customer's checks in the bank? _____

_____

3. What did Mr. McIver put on the sign in front of his store? _____

_____

4. How many bad checks has he been given since he put the sign up? Why? _____

_____

Fill in the blanks with words from the box.

1. How _____ did Mr. McIver lose?

2. What _____ of store did Mr. McIver have?

3. Some customers had _____ money to pay cash.

4. John hasn't seen anyone _____ yesterday.

5. How _____ pairs of shoes did Jim buy?

6. Mr. McIver has an appliance store. Does he sell anything _____ ?

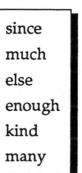

since

much

else

enough

kind

many

Use words from the story to complete the following sentences.

1. Mark wrote a check for $10. The check was sent back marked _____ because Mark only had $8.50 in his bank account.

2. John played a dirty trick on Frank. Now Frank wants his _____ .

3. Will you please _____ my paycheck when you go to the bank?

4. It is very expensive to take a case to _____ .

5. A good _____ does not write a bad check.

6. In the Afflecks' new house there are three _____ , a stove, refrigerator, and a washing machine.

Fill in the blanks with words from the box that mean the opposite.

1. long   _____
2. a lot   _____
3. front   _____
4. everyone   _____
5. put up   _____
6. bought   _____

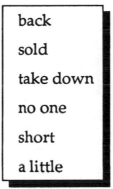

| |
| back |
| sold |
| take down |
| no one |
| short |
| a little |

Finish these sentences.

1. Last month Mr. McIver lost money because _____

_____

2. He didn't go to court because _____

_____

3. He put a sign up in front of his store because _____

_____

4. No one has given him a bad check since he put the sign up because _____

_____

Arrange the words in the following sentences in correct order. Write the corrected statement or question.

1. Mr. McIver / an appliance store. / owns

   _____

2. a lot of money / to court. / takes / to go / It

   _____

3. Mr. McIver's / are seventeen / names on / There / sign.

   _____

4. a bad / written / check? / you ever / Have

   _____

Use the following words to make your own sentences.

1. Mr. McIver / new store

   _____

2. customer / bad check

   _____

3. Mr. McIver / big sign

   _____

4. policeman / little boy

   _____

Fill in the blanks to complete the story. Try not to look back.

Mr. McIver has an _____ store. Some _____ his customers pay him _____ check. Last month several _____ gave him checks that _____ back. He lost _____ than $10,000.

The police _____ not help him. He _____ not go to court _____ that takes a long _____ and costs a lot _____ money. Instead, he put _____ sign in front of _____ store. He wrote the _____ of his bad customers _____ this sign. No one has _____ him a bad check since.

The Lucky Lottery Ticket

Vocabulary

carpenter	factory
lottery	draw
decide	

Have you ever bought a lottery ticket?

Have you ever won anything?

Amrik Gill is a carpenter. He works in a furniture factory. He has worked there for five years. He gets paid every two weeks. Last Friday he got paid. On payday Amrik always buys himself a lottery ticket. Last Friday he bought himself a lottery ticket at the store.

He said to the clerk, "One lottery ticket, please."

The clerk replied, "That will be one dollar, please."

"Here you are."

"Thank you," said the clerk with a smile. "Here's your lucky ticket."

"I hope so," said Amrik. "When is the drawing?"

"It's on Saturday." Amrik thanked the clerk and left the store.

On Saturday, Amrik and his wife stayed home. They both watched the drawing on TV. Amrik didn't win the million dollars, but he won $25,000. He jumped up and down and kissed his wife. Now they have to decide what to do with all their money.

Comprehension Questions

1. Where does Amrik Gill work? _____

   _____

2. What does Amrik do on payday? _____

   _____

3. How much did the lottery ticket cost? _____

   _____

4. Why did Amrik kiss his wife on Saturday? _____

   _____

Use words from the story to complete the following sentences.

1. A man who builds furniture is called a _____ .

2. Joanne forgot her umbrella. She was _____ that it didn't rain.

3. A _____ is not a sure way to make money.

4. It is hard to _____ where to go for a vacation.

Complete the following sentences with the correct form of the words in parentheses.

1. John won the race. He ran _____ than anyone else. (fast)

2. I will be the _____ person in the world if I win the lottery. (lucky)

3. Amrik worked _____ than any other worker in the factory. (hard)

4. Because they won money in the lottery, Amrik and his wife were _____ than their neighbors. (happy)

Complete the story by filling in the blanks.

Amrik Gill has _____ in a furniture factory for five _____ . Every _____ Amrik buys himself a lottery _____ . Last Friday he went to the store and _____ a lottery ticket. It _____ one dollar. The clerk smiled and said he hoped it would be a _____ ticket.

On the day of the _____ , Amrik and his wife stayed home. They _____ the drawing on TV. Amrik _____ $25,000. Now he and _____ wife have to decide _____ to do with the money that they won.

Composition

In the story there is a dialogue between Amrik and the clerk who sold him the lottery ticket. Rewrite it as a paragraph without the dialogue.

Example: He said to the clerk, "One lottery ticket, please."

Amrik asked the clerk for a lottery ticket.

_____

_____

_____

_____

_____

_____

_____

_____

_____

_____

A Problem

Vocabulary

problem	oldest
youngest	bookkeeper
assistant	mortgage payments
strangers	

Do you think a mother should work outside the home? Why?

John and Mary Smith have three small children. The oldest is three years old, and the youngest is nine months. John Smith is a bookkeeper. Mary Smith is a dental assistant. John and Mary want to buy a house, but they can't afford the mortgage payments. John wants Mary to go back to work. Mary wants to stay at home and look after the children. Both grandmothers live a long way from the Smiths, and Mary doesn't like to leave the children with strangers. She thinks that small children need their mother at home.

Comprehension Questions

1. How many children do John and Mary Smith have? _____

   _____

2. Why don't John and Mary buy a house? _____

   _____

3. What does John want Mary to do? _____

   _____

4. Who lives a long way from the Smiths? _____

   _____

5. Why doesn't Mary want to leave the children with strangers? _____

   _____

Complete the following sentences with the correct form of the words in parentheses.

1. John's _____ child is nine months old. (young)
2. Marion has four sisters. The _____ is fourteen. (old)
3. The trumpet is a _____ instrument than the flute. (noisy)
4. I know this path is narrow, but it gets _____ after we pass the waterfall. (narrow)
5. The next-door neighbor's grass is _____ than ours. (green)
6. Which of these five plums is the _____ ? (ripe)

Number the following sentences in order. Which happened first, second, and so on?

_____ Mary thinks that small children need their mother at home.
_____ Mary is a dental assistant.
_____ Mary's youngest child is nine months old.
       John wants Mary to go back to work.
_____ The children's grandmothers live a long way from them.
_____ Mary and John can't afford mortgage payments for a house.
_____ John is a bookkeeper.
_____ Mary doesn't like to leave the children with strangers.

Find three words in the box that fit with the following words. Write the three new compound words in the blanks.

1. book   _____   _____   _____

2. sales   _____   _____   _____

3. water   _____   _____   _____

4. some   _____   _____   _____

5. ice   _____   _____   _____

6. grand   _____   _____   _____

man	cream	keeper	fall	front	thing
skate	body	melon	shelf	clerk	stand
child	rink	tax	mother	case	one

Finish Mary's conversation with herself. Use words like _back to work, buy a house, grandmothers, strangers, children,_ and so on.

Mary: Oh dear! I would like to buy a house. John wants me to_____

          _____

          _____

          _____

          I don't know what to do!

Fill in the blanks to complete the story. Try not to look back.

The Smiths have three _____ . The oldest is three _____,
and the youngest is only _____ months. John Smith is _____
bookkeeper and his wife, _____ , is a dental assistant. _____
and Mary want to _____ a house, but they _____
afford the mortgage payments. _____ thinks Mary should go
_____ to work, but Mary _____ to stay home and
_____ after the children. Both _____ live a long way
_____ the Smiths, and Mary doesn't _____ to leave the
children _____ strangers. She thinks that _____
children need their mother _____ home.

18 A Very Wet Morning

Vocabulary

alarm	yawn
leaking	yell
waded	stretch
shocked	stuck

Have you ever been late for work or school? Why?

Yesterday morning, Jack woke up when his alarm clock rang. It was a gray, rainy day. He wanted to sleep a little longer, but he had to be at his office by nine o'clock. He had to get up. He yawned, stretched, and got out of bed. Immediately, he gave a loud yell. There was water all over the floor! Jack was shocked. He waded to the bathroom. The taps were leaking, and he couldn't turn them off because they were stuck. Jack had to call a plumber. Then he had to clean up his apartment. He was very late for work, but he had a good excuse. His boss didn't get mad at him.

Comprehension Questions

1. Why did Jack have to get up when his alarm clock rang? _____

   _____

2. Why did he yell when he got out of bed? _____

   _____

3. Why couldn't Jack turn off the leaking taps? _____

   _____

4. What did he do? _____

   _____

5. He was very late for work. What was his excuse? _____

   _____

Number the following sentences in order. Which happened first, second, and so on?

____ The taps were leaking, and Jack couldn't turn them off.
____ Jack yawned, stretched, and got out of bed.
____ Jack waded to the bathroom.
____ Yesterday morning, Jack woke up when his alarm clock rang.
____ Jack was shocked.
____ Jack had to call a plumber.
____ He was very late for work.
____ Jack gave a loud yell.
____ There was water on the floor.

Complete the following phrases with a form of the words in parentheses.

1. a little _____ (long)
2. a little _____ (soon)
3. a little _____ (early)
4. a little _____ (late)
5. a little _____ (near)
6. a lot _____ (happy)
7. a lot _____ (cheap)
8. a lot _____ (fast)
9. a lot _____ (friendly)
10. a lot _____ (young)

Use words from the story to complete the following sentences.

1. Fishermen often _____ in the river when they are fishing.
2. An unpleasant surprise can give you a nasty _____ .
3. Mary couldn't get the door open. It was _____ .
4. The people in the boat called for help because their boat was _____ .
5. Break the glass of the fire-_____ box with this ax.
6. I think Jimmy was very bored. He _____ all through the movie.

Finish the following conversation. Describe what has happened. Ask the plumber when he can come to fix the taps, and so on.

Jack: Hello? Is this the plumber?

Plumber: Yes. This is Pete the plumber. _____ ?

Jack: _____ ?

Plumber: _____

_____

_____

_____

_____

_____

Complete the following sentences.

1. The taps were leaking, so Jack

   _____ .

2. The traffic lights were red, so the cars

   _____ .

3. It was raining outside, so Jack

   _____ an umbrella.

4. It was too early to catch the plane, so Mary

   _____ .

5. The children were very hungry. There weren't any cookies in the house, so they

   _____ bread.

6. The plants were drying because it hadn't rained for a week, so the gardeners

   _____ them.

Fill in the blanks to complete the story. Try not to look back.

Yesterday morning, Jack woke _____ when his alarm clock _____ . It was a gray, _____ day. He wanted to _____ a little longer, but _____ had to be at _____ office by nine o'clock. He _____ to get up. He _____ , stretched, and got out _____ bed. Immediately, he gave _____ loud yell. There was _____ all over the floor. _____ was shocked. He waded _____ the bathroom. The taps _____ leaking, and he couldn't _____ them off because they _____ stuck. Jack had to _____ a plumber. Then he _____ to clean up his _____ . He was very _____ for work, but he _____ a good excuse. His _____ didn't get mad at _____ .

A Secondhand Car Lot

Vocabulary

smaller	afford
expensive	evening
overpriced	pushy

Have you ever bought a car?

Where did you buy it?

Bill's father wants a smaller car because the price of gas is getting higher. He can't afford to buy an expensive new car. Yesterday evening he went to a car lot to look at secondhand cars. He was angry because the cars were overpriced. He didn't like the salesman because he was too pushy. Today he told Bill, "I changed my mind. I'm going to get a new car."

They're going to look at some new cars this weekend.

Comprehension Questions

1. Why does Bill's father want a smaller car? _____

_____

2. Where did Bill's father go yesterday evening? _____

_____

3. Why was Bill's father angry? _____

_____

4. Why didn't he like the salesman? _____

_____

5. What are Bill and his father going to do this weekend? _____

_____

Circle the best ending for each sentence to agree with the story.

1. Bill's father
   a. can afford an expensive car.
   b. is too pushy.
   c. didn't like the salesman.
   d. is in the construction business.

2. The cars
   a. were new.
   b. were overpriced.
   c. were not for sale.
   d. all had flat tires.

3. The salesman
   a. sold Bill a car.
   b. sold Bill's father a car.
   c. plays soccer.
   d. was too pushy.

4. Bill
   a. is going with his father to look at new cars.
   b. thinks his father is too pushy.
   c. is going to buy a car.
   d. can't afford to buy a secondhand car.

Complete the following sentences with the correct form of the words in parentheses.

1. Bill's father has a big car. He is looking for a _____ one. (small)

2. He wants the _____ one he can find. (cheap)

3. The cars he saw were _____ than he wanted. (large)

4. The salesman was the _____ one on the lot. (pushy)

5. Bill's father is _____ than he has ever been before. (angry)

6. Bill and his father are _____ than they were before. (happy)

Write questions for the sentences below.

Example: John is sick because he has the flu.

   Why is John sick?

1. Bill's father wants a small car.

   What _____ ?

2. Bill's father went to a secondhand car lot to look at used cars.

   Why _____ ?

3. He was angry because the cars were overpriced.

   Why _____ ?

4. The salesman showed Bill's father a car that was too expensive.

   What _____ ?

5. Bill and his father are going to a car lot to see some new cars.

   Where _____ ?

Fill in the blanks to complete the story. Try not to look back.

Bill's father wants a _____ car because the price _____ gas is going up. _____ can't afford an expensive _____. Last night he _____ to a car lot _____ look at second-hand _____. He was angry. All _____ cars were overpriced. The _____ was pushy. Today Bill's _____ told Bill, "I've changed _____ mind. I'm going to _____ a new car."

_____ weekend they are going _____ look at some _____ cars.

The Traffic Offense

Vocabulary

hurry	patrol car	suddenly
nervously	sighed	also
points	behind	going

Have you ever been pulled over by the police?

How did you feel?

J anet was in a hurry. She had to meet her friend Nancy for lunch. She did not see the stop sign, but she did see the patrol car suddenly behind her. The policeman pulled her over. Janet waited nervously while he walked to her car. The policeman asked to see her driver's license. He took out his ticket book. Janet sighed. She was going to get a ticket, and she was also going to be late.

Comprehension Questions

1. Why was Janet in a hurry? _____

   _____

2. Who is Nancy? _____

   _____

3. What did Janet see behind her? _____

   _____

4. What did the policeman ask Janet? _____

   _____

5. What did the policeman do next? _____

   _____

6. Why did Janet sigh? _____

   _____

Complete the following sentences with the correct form of the words in parentheses.

1. Janet walked _____ . (quick)

2. Nancy waited _____ . (patient)

3. The car stopped _____ to let the boy cross the street. (sudden)

4. The children are playing _____ together. (happy)

5. The cat sniffed _____ around the new puppy. (curious)

6. She waited _____ at the window as the man walked toward the door. (nervous)

Pretend you are Janet or the Policeman. Write down the conversation between Janet and the Policeman.

Policeman: Did you see the stop sign?

Janet: I am sorry, I did not see the stop sign.

Policeman: _____

Janet: _____

Policeman: _____

Janet: _____

Policeman: _____

Janet: _____

Policeman: _____

Use words from the vocabulary to complete the following sentences.

1. Were you in a _____ yesterday?

2. She looked in the rearview mirror and saw a car right _____ her.

3. There is a _____ on the bridge with two policemen in it.

4. Tomorrow Robert is _____ to buy a new radio.

5. Bill got three _____ for driving across the Fifth Street bridge at ninety miles an hour.

6. Maria bought some ice cream at the store. She _____ bought a large bag of cookies.

Fill in the blanks to complete the story. Try not to look back.

Janet was on her _____ to meet Nancy for _____ .
She was in a _____ . She didn't see the _____ sign. She
drove past _____ without stopping. However, she _____
the patrol car suddenly _____ the rearview mirror. The _____
pulled her over. Janet _____ nervously while he walked _____
her car. He asked _____ see her driver's license. _____
took out his ticket _____ . Janet sighed. She was _____
to get a ticket. _____ was also going to _____ late for
lunch.

A Trip to the Dentist's Office

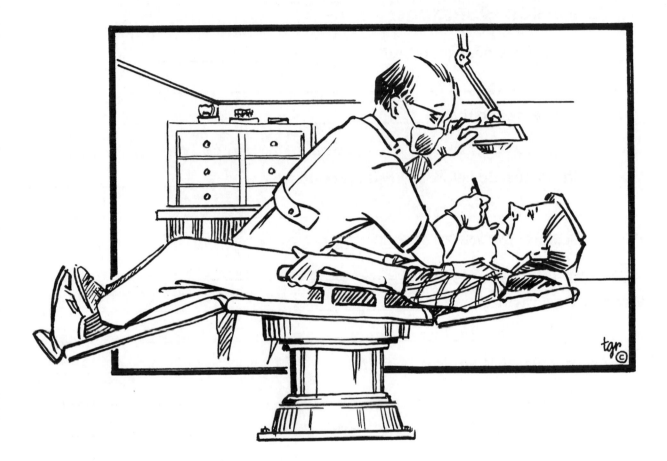

Vocabulary

dentist	cavities	hurt
jaw	injection	drill
terrible	ache	x-ray

How often do you go to the dentist?

Why do you go to the dentist?

Yesterday George went to the dentist's office because he had a terrible toothache. The dentist took x-rays of George's teeth and examined them.

"You have two large cavities," the dentist told George.

The dentist gave George an injection. He drilled the teeth, and then he filled them. George thanked the dentist. George didn't have a toothache, but his jaw ached all day.

Comprehension Questions

1. Why is George at the dentist's office? _____

   _____

2. What did the dentist do first? _____

   _____

3. What did the dentist do before he filled the cavities? _____

   _____

4. Why did George's jaw ache? _____

   _____

5. Why do we get cavities? _____

   _____

6. A dentist uses a drill. Who else uses a drill? _____

   _____

7. A dentist takes x-rays. Who else takes x-rays? _____

   _____

Use words from the vocabulary to complete the following sentences.

1. George has holes in his teeth. These are called _____ .
2. A dentist uses a special kind of _____ .
3. A doctor often _____ patients.
4. A skinned knee usually _____ at first.
5. There was a _____ thunderstorm last night.
6. George had a very sore _____ when he left the dentist's office.

Finish these sentences using *because*.

Example: George goes to the dentist.

because he has a toothache.

1. George doesn't mind having his tooth fixed

    _____

2. George has cavities

    _____

3. George can go home

    _____

Rewrite the story.

Yesterday I went to the dentist's office _____

_____

_____

_____

_____

_____

_____

_____

_____

Work with another student. Pretend you are the dentist and a patient. Some words you can use are *check-up, filling, extraction, appointment.* Write down your conversation.

Dentist: Good morning. How are you?

George: _____

Dentist: _____

_____

George: _____

Dentist: _____

George: _____

Write the letter of the word or phrase that best describes the meaning of *over* in the blank at the beginning of each sentence.

_____ 1. The boys jumped over the fence.

_____ 2. It has been over an hour since the bus left.

_____ 3. Mr. White hung the picture over the fireplace.

_____ 4. Can you reach over and turn off the stove?

_____ 5. When the movie was over, Marcia and Janet went to have a cup of coffee.

_____ 6. Indra came over after dinner.

_____ 7. There were six blueberry muffins left over after everyone finished breakfast.

a. to my house

b. finished, ended

c. across

d. from one side to another

e. above

f. remaining

g. more than

A Bad Job Experience

Vocabulary

experience   student

several   busperson

willing   hummed

Have you ever worked in a restaurant?

What did you do? What's the best job you ever had?

When Viet Minh was a student, he lived in San Francisco. He needed a part-time job because he didn't have any money. He looked for a job for several weeks. One day he saw a sign in the window of a restaurant. It said "Busperson wanted." He went into the restaurant and spoke to the manager.

The manager asked him, "Do you have any experience as a busperson?"

Viet Minh said, "No, but I'm willing to work very hard."

The manager said, "You are hired."

Viet Minh was very happy to have the job. For one hour he worked very hard and very fast. He thought he would be the restaurant's best busperson. He hummed a song while he worked. As soon as the customers finished their food, he took away the dishes and cleaned the tables. Sometimes he even took away the dishes before the customers were finished.

The manager said to Viet Minh, "You work too well. You are fired."

Comprehension Questions

1. Where did the man in the story live when he was a student? _____

   _____

2. Why did he need a job? _____

   _____

3. Why did the manager hire him if he didn't have any experience? _____

   _____

4. What does a busperson in a restaurant do? _____

   _____

5. Why did he get fired? _____

   _____

Number the following sentences in order. Which happened first, second, and so on?

_____² He needed a job because he didn't have any money.

_____³ The manager hired him.

_____⁴ There was a sign that said "Busperson Wanted" in the window.

_____ Viet Minh was happy to have the job.

_____ Sometimes he even took the dishes before the customers were finished.

_____ He worked very hard and very fast.

_____ The manager said, "You are fired."

_____¹ When Viet Minh was a student, he lived in San Francisco.

Use words from the story to complete the following sentences.

1. Would you be _____ to mow the grass for five dollars?

2. He needs a salesman with _____ .

3. Jim got a job as a _____ .

4. At last! I have _____ my homework.

5. There are _____ books on that table.

6. Six other _____ are in my English class.

7. My mother liked music. She always _____ while she did the house-work.

Find the meaning for each word and circle the letter.

1. experience
   a. knowledge or skill
   b. a test
   c. costs a lot

2. student
   a. a place where an artist works
   b. someone who goes to school
   c. hard-working

3. willing
   a. ready and glad
   b. full of water
   c. written by a lawyer

4. busperson
   a. driver of a bus
   b. someone who works in a restaurant
   c. a mechanic

5. several
   a. a lot
   b. a few
   c. cut

Fill in the blanks with the letter of the description that best matches the job.

____ 1. pilot   a. works in a bank
____ 2. busperson   b. mends shoes
____ 3. teller   c. works in the woods
____ 4. secretary   d. flies planes
____ 5. shoemaker   e. works in a restaurant
____ 6. logger   f. works in an office

Fill in the blanks to complete the story. Try not to look back.

When Viet Minh was _____ student, he lived in _____.
He needed a part-time _____ because he didn't have _____
money. He looked for _____ job for several weeks. _____
day he saw a _____ that said, "Busperson Wanted" in the
_____ of a restaurant. He _____ into the restaurant and
_____ to the manager.

"Do _____ have any experience as _____
busperson?" the manager asked _____ .

"No, but I'm willing _____ work very hard."

The _____ told him he was _____ . Viet Minh was
very _____ to have the job. _____ one hour he worked
very hard and very fast. _____ thought he would be _____
restaurant's best busperson. He _____ a song while he _____.
As soon as the _____ had finished their food, _____
took the dishes away _____ cleaned the tables. Sometimes
_____ even took the dishes _____ before the customers
were _____ .

"You work too well," _____ the manager said to _____.
"You are fired."

23 Koji Complains

Vocabulary

complain   stereo

neighbors   rude

mind   upset

Have you ever had noisy neighbors?

What would you do if your neighbors were too noisy?

Koji lives in a new apartment building. The walls of his apartment are very thin.

Koji is a mail carrier. He must get up early in the mornings to go to work. He usually goes to bed at 11:15 PM. Last night, his neighbors downstairs had a big party. They played loud rock music. At two o'clock in the morning he went downstairs. He knocked on his neighbor's door. Koji asked his neighbor to turn his stereo down. The man at the door was very rude to him. He told Koji to mind his own business. He shut the door in Koji's face.

Koji was very upset. He didn't get to sleep until four o'clock. The next morning he complained to the manager of the building. The manager said, "I will talk to those people."

Comprehension Questions

1. Where does Koji live? _____

_____

2. When does he usually go to bed? _____

_____

3. Why couldn't he sleep last night? _____

_____

4. What did he do at two o'clock in the morning? _____

_____

5. What did he do the next morning? _____

_____

Circle the correct word in parentheses to make the sentence agree with the story.

1. The people who live _____ had a party. (next door, downstairs)

2. They were very _____ . (quiet, noisy)

3. Koji was _____ when the neighbors were rude to him. (sick, upset)

4. His neighbors were making a _____ of noise. (lot, little)

5. The man told Koji to _____ . (come to the party, go away and leave them alone).

Write the word from the box that means the opposite of the underlined word in the sentence.

Example: Koji _always_ goes to bed early. _____ *never* _____

1. Koji was very <u>polite</u>.   _____

2. Koji is late for work.   _____

3. The neighbor <u>shut</u> the door quickly. _____

4. The walls of the apartment were <u>thin</u>.   _____

5. <u>The next morning</u> Koji complained. _____

yesterday	early	rude
thick	opened	never

Rewrite the following sentences.

Example: "Be quiet!" Bill said to his neighbor.

   Bill told his neighbor to be quiet. _____

1. "Will you take the garbage out?" Mr. Jones asks his daughter. _____

   _____

2. Aunt Jane said, "Go to bed at once, Eva." _____

   _____

3. "Please make less noise," Koji asks the man downstairs. _____

   _____

4. "Feed the dog once a day while we are away, James," Mr. Naylor told the sitter. ___

   _____

5. "Come with us on the picnic, Granny," Alan said to his grandmother. _____

   _____

6. "I want the front door painted light green," Mrs. Sales tells the painter's helper. ___

   _____

Use words from the story to complete the following sentences.

1. Jane had a fight with her sister yesterday. Today she feels _____ about it.

2. On July 4 there is _____ a display of fireworks.

3. The policeman was _____ to Mrs. Jones when she asked him where to pay her parking ticket.

4. The tap kept dripping, so I _____ to the landlord.

5. She sent Margaret to borrow some sugar from the _____ .

Fill in the blanks to complete the story. Try not to look back.

Koji lives in a _____ apartment building. The walls _____ the apartment are very _____ .

Koji is a mail carrier. _____ must get up early _____ go to work. He _____ goes to bed at _____ . Last night his neighbors _____ had a big party. _____ played loud rock music. _____ two o'clock in the morning Koji went downstairs _____ knocked on his neighbor's _____ . He asked his neighbor _____ turn the stereo down. _____ man was very rude _____ told Koji to mind _____ own business. He shut _____ door in Koji's face.

_____ was very upset. He _____ get to sleep until _____ . The next morning he _____ to the manager. The _____ said he would talk _____ the neighbors.

Flight Arrangements

Vocabulary

flight	arrangements	connecting
confirm	expensive	direct
ago	restaurant	departure
travel agent	replied	anniversary
reservations	must	

Do you like to travel?

Where have you traveled in the United States?

How do you like to travel?

Amarjit wants to fly to Los Angeles tomorrow. Three days ago he went to the Exotic Holiday Travel Agency. The travel agent said, "I'm sorry, Mr. Sandhu, but there isn't a direct flight to Los Angeles on Tuesdays."

"I must travel to Los Angeles on Tuesday," said Amarjit. "My parents are having their fiftieth wedding anniversary, and I want to take them to an expensive restaurant for dinner."

"You can still fly to Los Angeles on Tuesday," the travel agent replied, "but you have to take two planes. You must fly to Chicago first. Then you have to take a connecting flight to Los Angeles."

Amarjit was very happy. He made reservations for a seat yesterday. Today he's going to phone the airline's reservation desk. He wants to confirm his reservation. Everything is fine. Amarjit has to check in at the airport an hour before departure time. He is going to pay for his ticket at the airport.

Comprehension Questions

1. Why does Amarjit want to fly to Los Angeles on Tuesday? _____

    _____

2. What does he want to do on his parent's fiftieth wedding anniversary? _____

    _____

3. How will Amarjit get to Los Angeles? _____

    _____

4. Where does he phone to confirm his reservations? _____

    _____

5. Where does he pay for his ticket? _____

    _____

6. When should Amarjit check in at the airport? _____

    _____

Write *true* or *false* at the beginning of each sentence.

_____ 1. There is no direct flight to Los Angeles on Tuesday.
_____ 2. Amarjit can't get to Los Angeles in time for his parent's anniversary.
_____ 3. Amarjit does not need reservations on the plane.
_____ 4. He will fly to Chicago and then to Los Angeles.
_____ 5. He pays for his ticket at the travel agent's office.
_____ 6. It took six days to get a reservation.
_____ 7. Amarjit must check in at the airport at least an hour before departure time.

Use two words from the box to fill in the blanks in each sentence.

1. Today is my _____ _____ .
2. We are going to an _____ _____ .
3. My uncle used to be a _____ _____ .
4. Amarjit wanted a _____ _____ to Los Angeles.
5. Bettina works at the _____ _____ of U.S. Air.
6. What is the _____ _____ of the flight to San Diego?

travel	departure	time	reservation
direct	desk	expensive	restaurant
agent	anniversary	wedding	flight

Pretend you are Amarjit. Write a letter to your parents telling them that you are coming to Los Angeles for their wedding anniversary. Ask them to dinner at a restaurant.

_____

_____

_____

_____

_____

_____

_____

Fill in the blanks to complete the story. Try not to look back.

Amarjit wants to fly _____ Los Angeles tomorrow. Three days _____ he went to the _____ Holiday Travel Agency. The _____ agent told him that _____ is no direct _____ to Los Angeles on Tuesdays. Amarjit told the travel agent that he _____ to get to Los Angeles on _____ because it is his parents' fiftieth wedding anniversary. He _____ to take them to _____ expensive restaurant for dinner.

"_____ can still fly to _____ on Tuesday," the travel _____ replied, "but you have to _____ two planes. You fly _____ Chicago first and then _____ a connecting flight to _____ ."

Amarjit was very happy. _____ made reservations for a _____ yesterday. Today he's phoning _____ airlines reservation desk to _____ his reservation. Everything is _____ . Amarjit must check in _____ the airport an _____ before departure time. He _____ going to pay for _____ ticket at the airport.

 # Mrs. Pratt's Bus Trip

Vocabulary

kind	forgets	rush hour
traffic	hurry	reaches
still	lost and found	turn in

Have you ever left anything on a bus or train?

What did you do?

Mrs. Pratt is very kind to friends. She never forgets their birthdays. Today is Mrs. Pratt's day off. It is also her best friend's birthday. Mrs. Pratt is going to see her. She is taking a birthday cake. At the bus stop there are long lines of people. They all want to get on the bus. It is rush hour. The bus is very slow because there is a lot of traffic. Mrs. Pratt is late. She gets off the bus in a great hurry. When she reaches her friend's door, she remembers that the cake is still on the bus. Her friend tells her not to worry and goes to the phone. She phones the Lost and Found office of Regional Transit. The man at the office tells her to phone tomorrow morning. If they find the cake on the bus, Mrs. Pratt can pick it up at the Lost and Found office at 696 28th Street between nine AM and five PM.

Comprehension Questions

1. What is Mrs. Pratt doing on her day off? _____

   _____

2. Why is Mrs. Pratt late? _____

   _____

3. What does she remember *after* she gets off the bus? _____

   _____

4. Her friend makes a phone call. Whom does she phone? _____

   _____

5. What does the man at the office say? _____

   _____

6. When can Mrs. Pratt pick up the cake if it is at the Lost and Found office? _____

   _____

7. The title of this story is "Mrs. Pratt's Bus Trip." What other title can you think of for it? _____

   _____

Write *true* or *false* at the beginning of each sentence.

_____ 1.   Mrs. Pratt forgot to buy a birthday cake.
_____ 2.   There are long lines of people at the bus stop.
_____ 3.   The Lost and Found office is open from nine AM to five PM.
_____ 4.   Mrs. Pratt left her purse on the bus.
_____ 5.   The bus is in a great hurry.
_____ 6.   Mrs. Pratt is taking today off work because she isn't feeling well.
_____ 7.   Her friend is upset because Mrs. Pratt didn't bring her a cake.

Complete the following sentences with the correct form of the words in parentheses.

1. The bus goes _____ in rush-hour traffic. (slow)

2. Mrs. Pratt waits _____ . (impatient)

3. The driver talks _____ to the boy. (rude)

4. A tall, thin policeman walks _____ toward Mrs. Pratt. (quick)

5. He shouts _____ . (angry)

6. Please walk _____ . The baby is asleep. (quiet)

Arrange the words in the following sentences in correct order. Write the corrected statement or question.

1. there long lines / at the bus stop? / of people / Why are / waiting _____

    _____

2. the Lost and Found office is / number of / 663-2133. / The telephone _____

    _____

3. birthday cake / Poor / on the bus. / Mrs. Pratt / left the _____

    _____

4. of exams. / the first day / Today is _____

    _____

5. cars / across the / each day? / Golden Gate bridge / How many / drive _____

    _____

Mrs. Pratt knocks on her friend's door. The friend opens it. Write a conversation between Mrs. Pratt and her friend using the words *birthday, a lot of traffic, left, cake, bus, worry, Lost and Found,* **and so on.**

_____

_____

_____

_____

_____

_____

_____

_____

_____

_____

Fill in the blanks to complete the story. Try not to look back.

Mrs. Pratt is kind _____ her friends. She never _____ their birthdays. Today is _____ day off. It is _____ her best friend's birthday. _____ Pratt is going to _____ her. She is taking _____ birthday cake. At the _____ there are long lines _____ people who want to _____ on the bus. It _____ rush hour. The bus is _____ slow because there is _____ lot of traffic. Mrs. _____ is late. She gets _____ the bus in a hurry. When she reaches her friend's house, she remembers _____ she left the cake _____ the bus! Her friend _____ the Lost and Found office. _____ man at the office _____ her that if they _____ the cake on the _____ , Mrs. Pratt can pick _____ up between nine AM and _____ .

Appendix

Guide to Major Verb Tenses and Grammatical Structures in Each Story

Story	Verb Tenses	Grammatical Structures
1. Sour Milk	Past Present	Comparison Classifiers of nouns
2. Paying by Check	Present Past	Indirect objects
3. The Old Car	Present	Possessives (nouns and pronouns)
4. Julie's Job Worries	Present	Cause/effect clause
5. Chinese New Year	Present Present continuous	Indefinite pronouns (*nothing/nobody*)
6. The Lost Child	Present Past	Compound words Adjectives
7. Bobby's Adventure	Present	Alphabetizing
8. House Hunting	Present Past	Present continuous Present participle
9. The Christmas Party	Past Present	Compound words Reflexive pronouns
10. Mr. Specogna's Success	Past	Infinitives Prepositions Alphabetical order Frequency adverbs
11. Mrs. Wong's Visit to the Laundromat	Past Present	Alphabetical order
12. All He Wanted Was a Glass of Water	Past Present	Adverbs Adverbial phrases

Story	Verb Tenses	Grammatical Structures
13. Change of Address	Past Present Future	Adverbs of time Comparison
14. Blood Donors	Present	Prepositions
15. Mr. McIver's Revenge	Past Present	Nouns Adjectives Adverbs Opposites
16. The Lucky Lottery Ticket	Present Past	Comparison
17. A Problem	Present	Infinitives Comparison Compound words
18. A Very Wet Morning	Past	Comparison using *a lot / a little / had to*
19. A Secondhand Car Lot	Present Past	Comparison
20. The Traffic Offense	Past Present	Adverbs
21. A Trip to the Dentist's Office	Past Present	Cause/effect clause
22. A Bad Job Experience	Past Present Future	Direct quotations Opposites
23. Koji Complains	Present Past	Indirect quotations
24. Flight Arrangements	Present Past Future	Adjectives/nouns
25. Mrs. Pratt's Bus Trip	Present	Adverbs